Samuel Ives Curtiss

The Name Machabee

Samuel Ives Curtiss

The Name Machabee

ISBN/EAN: 9783337144265

Printed in Europe, USA, Canada, Australia, Japan

Cover: Foto ©ninafisch / pixelio.de

More available books at **www.hansebooks.com**

THE NAME MACHABEE

BY

SAMUEL IVES CURTISS, Jr.,

DOCTOR OF PHILOSOPHY, LEIPZIG.

LEIPZIG,

J. C. HINRICHS.

1876.

CONTENTS.

INTRODUCTION.

NAMES are crystallized history and poetry, or to change the simile they are the embalmed remains of warm affections, bitter griefs, ardent hopes and lofty aspirations. As the discovery of a single bone may enable the naturalist to reconstruct the skeleton of an animal belonging to some long extinct species, so the recovery of an ancient name often enables the historian to represent to the imagination the living men and women of the past.

There is a peculiar charm in the study of the earlier Hebrew names arising from the artless character of the people, which led them to make their children the remembrancers of their joys and their sorrows, their failures and their successes. Indeed in this respect the several crises of the Jewish history are marked by the same phenomena as its beginning, so that a single name sometimes supplies a missing link, and gives a hint of the popular feeling which otherwise would be entirely wanting.

Whether we regard the names of the Hebrews from a *romantic, philologic* or a *historic* point of view, we are equally impressed with their importance. What more fruitful theme for the imagination than the names of the early patriarchs! The experiences of these ancient families are gathered up and preserved in the names of the children. If all other records were to perish, we should still have in *Abraham* the founder of a nation, in *Isaac* the laughter of joyous parents,

1

and in *Jacob* one of the shrewdest characters in sacred history.

Viewed from a philologic point of view, words and forms have been preserved to us in these names, which otherwise would have been entirely lost, which belong either to the earliest period of the language or to some foreign tongue. [1])

But nowhere are the Hebrew names of greater importance than for the history of the people. Whether we contemplate that large class of names which stamp the Israelites as a nation whose God is the Lord, or those which record their sojourn in a strange land, or those which are a recognition of the divine wrath, or a memorial of returning hope, gratitude and joy, we have abundant testimony to the value of this much neglected department of study, and we find that the long lists in the Chronicles are replete with interest.

It is true that doubt and uncertainty attend the investigation of many names which have become changed almost beyond recognition through the attrition of time; nevertheless patient research unlocks many a secret and is at all times a blessing to him who engages in it.

I am aware of the dangers to which one in pursuing a subject of this kind is exposed. It is easier to theorize than to examine, and one is often, especially in such a case, carried captive by some attractive theory, which is merely an exhalation of the imagination.

---

1) Examples of words preserved in proper names are קְדָה and חֵרָה; of old forms, the nominative ending of חֲמוּ in חֲמוּטַל, the genitive in אֲבִישָׁלוֹם, and the original feminine ending *at* in בְּשָׂמַת; of words belonging to the earliest period of the language, רָחָם in אַבְרָחָם, and צֵצִי; and of foreign words, the more Persian than Hebrew פַּרְנָךְ and the first Aramaic part of the compound in מְשֵׁיזַבְאֵל.

I have tried to leave no stone unturned in this investigation. I have entered into correspondence with all the principal libraries in Europe, and through the great courtesy of their distinguished custodians I am able to present some facts, which have hitherto escaped notice, and to fully vindicate the claim to original investigation.

While engaged in collecting these materials a shadow has flitted across my path, as I have thought that some might consider the subject unworthy of such research, and might in view of my performance repeat the familiar verse:

Parturiunt montes, nascetur ridiculus mus.

But if men can die for an idea, if a single word can gather in itself the longings, the aspirations and the hopes of generations, if some names have gained an immortal fame and have become synonymous of all that is noblest and best in this world, then the name of the great hero and devout patriot who was the first to cross one of the darkest skies of Jewish history with a brilliance which arrested every eye, whether of friend or foe, his name, I say, given at such a period and by such a people is worthy of the most patient research and the most studious consideration.

Whether it shall be my lot to determine the true meaning of this name, I trust that the following discussion may not be without advantage to all who are interested in the critical study of the Machabaean history.

4

I.

The chief difficulty in the discussion of this subject has been occasioned by the loss of the original Hebrew[1]) text of the first book of Machabees, which would be decisive as to the letters which compose the name. For more than twelve hundred years it and all similar memorials[2]) have disappeared from view. In the absence of direct testimony we must accept the deposition of those who saw the ancient Hebrew MS. But here again we are met

---

1) That the original text was Hebrew, appears *1)* from historical testimony: Jerome in the Prologus Galeatus (Biblia Sacra Latina ed. Heyse et Tischendorf, Lipsiae 1873, p. XXVIII) says: *Machabaeorum primum librum hebraicum reperi.* Moreover Origen is quoted by Eusebius Lib. VI Cap. 25 as saying: Ἔξω δὲ τούτων ἐστὶ τὰ Μακκαβαϊκὰ, ἅπερ ἐπιγέγραπται Σαρβὴθ Σαρβανιέλ, see Appendix 1 of this Dissertation. *2)* There is strong internal evidence of a Hebrew original. Comp. Grimm, „Das erste Buch der Maccabäer", S. XV. 4. who cites I. 16, 36; II. 57; III. 9, 32; IV. 3, 13, 17 f. as examples of a slavish imitation of the Hebrew, and I. 28; II. 8, 34; III. 3; IV. 19, 24; comp. XI 28; XIV. 5; XVI. 3 which only become clear by presupposing mistakes in translation.

2) The *Halachoth gedoloth*, which according to Zunz „Die gottesdienstlichen Vorträge der Juden, Berlin 1832" p. 124 might have been composed about the eighth century, mentions the *Megillath bêth-Chashmonaë* in the section, entitled Hilchoth Sofrim (f. 83 column 3 ed. Zolkiew), as follows:

זקני בית שמאי וזקני בית הילל חם כחבו מגלת בית חשמונאי ועד עכשיו
לא עלה לדורות עד שיעמוד כהן לאורים ותומים:

"*The elders of the house of Shammai and the elders of the house of Hillel wrote the Megillath of the Hasmonean family, but till now it has been lost (and will not be found) until a priest shall arise with the Urim and Thummim.*"

with a very serious difficulty. The testimony, like
some of the responses of the ancient Delphic Oracle,
is on the first blush equivocal. It is necessary first
of all to know the Hebrew letters of which the name
Μακκαβαῖος is composed. The entire discussion will
largely turn upon the original form of the second
letter. Shall we read מקבי or מכבי? If unanimity,
the weight of great names, an attractive etymology
and a striking historical parallel could settle any
question, then we must accept מקבי as the true reading. It is certain however that the question cannot
be settled in this way, hence it is necessary that it
should be exposed to the most searching criticism.

There are two witnesses who saw the Hebrew
original. The one is the Greek translator, the other
Jerome. In determining the weight and relative importance of their testimony we must first consider
their character and antecedents. In the absence of
the original, it is impossible to judge of the merits
of the Greek translator, as we can of those of the
LXX. It is not probable that in point of accuracy
he would be superior to any of the various Alexandrian translators of the canonical books of the Old
Testament. If we add to this the comparatively easy
and flowing Greek style[1]) in which the book is
written, in spite of its Hebraisms, we certainly need
not be surprised if some names, through the transcription, have almost entirely lost their Hebrew character, to say nothing of the errors of copyists.

We can however form a correct opinion in regard to the attainments of Jerome as a Hebrew
scholar, the merits of his translation and his accu-

1) Comp. Grimm l. c. §. XV.

racy in details. Though his knowledge of Hebrew was very imperfect as judged by the present standard, he was by far the most advanced in the language of any of fathers, and his translation is of great critical value [1]). He often gives the Hebrew names much more accurately than the Alexandrian translators. [2]) We know, from a comparison of the proper names, what his system of rendering the Hebrew letters is — I say system because he does not vary in his orthography like the Rabbinical transcribers of Greek and Latin words. [3]) He frequently corrects the errors which appear in the LXX. Although the first book of Machabees is not canonical, there can be no doubt that he would carefully transcribe the name since he informs us that he has found it in Hebrew. [4])

---

1) Comp. Nowack, „Die Bedeutung des Hieronymus." Göttingen, 1875 (See especially p. 55).

2) It is certain that Jerome adheres much more closely to the present Hebrew text in his transcription of names than the LXX. The most natural supposition is that he conformed the Latin translation of the LXX to the Hebrew original. For a comparative view of the transcription of proper names by the LXX and Jerome see appendix II.

3) See appendix III.

4) Granted that Jerome left the old Latin translation of 1. Machab. untouched, and that he simply used the current spelling of the name, we have in this an indication, that *chi* or single *kappa* stood in the Greek text from which the Latin was translated, since the Latin translator would never transcribe double *kappa* through *ch*. Yet I do not grant it, as I can not accept Sabatier's and Fritzsche's opinion that Jerome left the old Latin translation unchanged. I believe that the translation of the St. Germain MS., which Sabatier gives, is a part of the original Latin translation which was adopted by Jerome after some emendations. Grimm's view that the translation of the St. Germain MS. is the effort of a later period to

It is not probable that he would make such a
discovery without at least using it to give the correct spelling of the name. When we compare the
testimony of these two witnesses, it seems at first
to be contradictory. The Greek spells the name
Μακκαβαῖος, which most simply and naturally corresponds to מקבי, while Jerome spells the name *Machabaeus*, which is equivalent to מכבי. Is there a real
contradiction here, or can the two be reconciled?
It is possible that in the MS. which was accessible
to the Greek translator the name was written with
koph and in that which was found by Jerome with
kaph? If however this name was originally written
with *koph*, it is unlikely that it would afterwards be
written with *kaph*. It is most probable that both
the Greek and Jerome read either מקבי or מכבי.
Let us test the two readings. *Machabaeus* cannot
be the transcription of מקבי, since it is entirely contrary to the usage of Jerome to transcribe *koph*
with *ch*.

1. He always renders *koph* with *c*. Out of the
one hundred and ninety names written with *koph*,
which I have repeatedly examined, there are only
two *apparently* established exceptions[1]), which cannot
be counted as such upon examination.

2. He carefully distinguishes between forms ending in *koph* and *kaph*. See the proper names

secure a more literal translation than the Vulgate is higly improbable. Fritzsche strikes at the root of the matter when he says of
the St. Germain Version "Est antiquior, genere dicendi horridior et
verborum textus Graeci tenacior." Libri Apocr. V. T. p. XX.

1) Jerome transcribes יְחֶזְקֵאל through *Ezechiel* 1 Ch. XXIV, 16;
and יְחִזְקִיָּהוּ through *Ezechias* 2 Ch. XXVIII, 12. The *ch* in these
cases has arisen from the euphonic transposition of the letters.

שִׁישַׁק *Sesac* I. Ch. VIII, 14; שִׁישַׁה *Sesach* Jer. XXV, 26; שׁוֹבֵק *Sobec* Nehem. X, 25 (26); שׁוֹבַךְ *Sobach* 2. Sam. X, 16; comp. עַרְקִי *Arcaeus* Gen. X, 17 and אַרְבִּי *Arachites* 2 Sam. XV, 32.

3. He rigidly indicates the distinction between names which begin with מק and those which begin with מכ. Comp. מָקֵץ *Macces* 1 Kings IV, 9; מִקֵּדָה *Maceda* Josh. X, 10 with מַכְבַּנַּי *Machbanai* 1 Ch. XII, 13 and מִבְרִי *Mochori* 1 Ch. IX, 8.

4. Since it is a fixed law of Jerome's tran-scription, that *koph* always equals *c* and never *ch*, and supposing that *Macabeus* was at first written for מקבי and that it must be changed for the sake of euphony, an *h* would not be inserted after *Mac*: *Mac(h)abeus*, but the *c* would be doubled[1]) e. g. מקץ *Macces* 1. K. IV, 9; עֶקְרוֹן *Accaron* Josh. XV, 45; רִבְקָה *Rebecca* Gen. XXII, 23. Hence *Machabeus* cannot have come from מקבי.

On the other hand however Μαχχαβαῖος can have arisen from מכבי.

1. While the LXX generally transcribe *kaph* with *chi*, there are several instances in wich they render it with *kappa*. E. g. כְּפִירָה Κεφιρά Josh. XVIII, 26 (24); בְּתִּים Κήτιοι Gen. X, 4; כַּרְמֶל Κάρμηλος Jer. XLVI, 18; סַבְתְּכָא Σαβαθαχά Gen. X, 7; שֵׁכָר σίκερα (frequently) and שׁוֹבַךְ Σωβάχ 2 Sam. X, 16.

2. מכבי might have been transcribed at first through Μαχαβαῖος. This could afterwards have been changed undesignedly to Μαχχαβαῖος, since the *kappa* was involuntarily doubled through a more rapid pro-

---

1) We have an example of this euphonic doubling in the later form *Macchabeus*. Comp. *Sychaeus*, Συχαῖος, which in later MSS. is written *Sycchaeus*.

nunciation. Very many cases of similar doubling occur. E. g. מִתְקָה Μαθεκκά Numb. XXXIII, 28; אֱמֹרִי 'Αμορραῖος; שֶׁמִיר Σεμμήρ 1 Ch. VIII, 12; יָפוֹ 'Ιόππη; אֲבִישָׁלוֹם 'Αβεσσαλώμ. In the three or four hundred years which elapsed between the translation of I. Machabees from the Hebrew and our oldest Greek MSS. Μαχαβαῖος could very easily have become Μακκαβαῖος. One case at least occurs in which the Greek translator has transcribed *kaph* through double *kappa*, viz. תֹּבֶךְ Θοκκά 1 Ch. IV, 32.[1]) I hold therefore that Jerome's transcription indicates מכבי as the original form, and that there is nothing to hinder the derivation of the Greek from it.

The evidence of the other witnesses, although often cited, is of so little weight in the treatment of this question that I should not cite them except to illustrate this statement and the further discussion of this subject. They are 1. *the Syriac version;* 2. *Jusippon ben Gurion;* 3. *the Megillath Antiochos;* and 4. *the second so called book of Machabees in Arabic.*

1. It has been proved beyond the shadow of a doubt that the Syriac is a translation from the Greek[2]). The fact that the Syrian writes the name with *koph* ܡܟܒܝ merely shows that he regarded single *kappa* and especially double *kappa* as the equivalent of *koph* without considering how it had arisen.

2. Jusippon ben Gurion has often been quoted as an authority. His reading of the name is מכבאי or according to other MSS. מבבי. Since this Hebrew

---

1) As a rule letters are often doubled in the later MSS. which are single in the earlier.

2) Comp. Trendelenburg, Repertorium für biblische und morgenländische Litteratur Theil 15 S. 60. See such examples as ἐπὶ τὴν 'Ελλάδα ܕ...܇ 1 Machab. I, 1.

Jusippon did not appear before the tenth century[1]), and the Hebrew MS. of first Machabees was lost long before, his reading of the word seems to indicate that he has merely reproduced Jerome's transcription *Machabaeus*. This is highly probable, for his writings seem to indicate that he had scarcely any knowledge of Greek and that his home was in Italy. His sources have been characterized by Zunz as *translations of translations*.[2])

3. If we now turn to the reading of the name as it occurs in the different MSS. of the Aramean and Hebrew Megillath Antiochos (which is also called the מגלה יונית, the Greek Megilla), we shall find that two modes of spelling are in vogue מכבי and מקבי with a preponderance in favor of the latter. Since the name does not occur in either of the Talmuds[3]) we can only hold that this מכבי or מקבי of the Megilla is the transcription of the name from the Latin or Greek.[4]) The transcription מקבי could come from the

---

1) Zunz, Die gottesdienstlichen Vorträge der Juden, S. 146—154, Comp. Gesammelte Schriften, Band 2 (1875), S. 159 ff.

2) Comp. Zunz, Die gottesdienstlichen Vorträge, S. 149.

3) Neither the name מכבי nor מקבי occurs in the Gemara. So far as they are found in later Jewish writings, they have either been derived from Hellenistic or Latin sources. The names which occur in the Mishna although somewhat resembling the above are foreign to the Hebrew and have no connection with this name. Compare the appellative הַמַּקְבָן (Hammer-head i. e. one whose head resembles a hammer) in the Mishna Bechoroth VII. 1 (Gemara 43ᵇ) and the proper name מגבאי in the proverb: *Sichem is married and Magbai is circumcised*, see Buxtorfii Lex. Rabb. p. 2392 under שכם. Zunz, *Namen der Juden* 1837 (in his *Gesammelte Schriften*, Band 2, 1876) combines the names מגבי and מחבי with the name Machabee, but without adducing any reasons.

4) See Appendix V.

Greek mediately through the Syriac, especially if we hold that the reading מיקבי in these MSS. is of oriental origin. This conjecture seems to be substantiated by the form wich is given to this name in two MSS. of the Royal Berlin library which came from Yemen, and which are punctuated according to the Babylonian system.[1]) On the other hand those who wrote the name מכבי, undoubtedly followed the Latin orthography. It must however be remarked, that while Jerome renders *koph* by *c* there are a few cases in later Hebrew, in which *ch* is rendered with *koph*, e. g. כרטס or קרטס is written for *charta*.[2]) Hence it is possible that the transcription with *koph* has merely risen from *ch* through the carelessness or ignorance of the transcriber, although it is more probable that it has arisen from the Greek. It will, I think, be fully seen that the testimony of these MSS. proves nothing either way.

4. The Arabic second book of Machabees [3]) (كتاب المقابيّين وهو الثّانى), which traces the Jewish history from the attempted seizure of the treasures in the temple by Heliodorus until nearly the birth of Christ, is apparently derived more or less remotely from the Greek sources. The title as it simply rests upon a transcription is utterly without significance for this discussion.

I claim therefore as the result of this survey:
1. that neither the Megillath Antiochos nor the Arabic second book of Machabees are to be regarded in this discussion, since they only give indirect transcriptions;
2. that the testimony of the Greek translator and Je-

---

1) See Appendix VI. 2) See Appendix III.
3) It is to be found in the London Polyglott Tom. IV p. 112—59.

rome is of paramount importance; 3. that while Machabeus could not have come from מקבי, both Μαχχαβαῖος
and Machabeus can have arisen from מכבי which I
adopt as the correct reading.

II.

Having fixed upon the original reading of the
name, it now remains to consider its signification. Before presenting my own idea I whish to consider the
various explanations which have ben suggested.

The earliest hint at the meaning of the name was
given by Jusippon ben Gurion, where he represents
the dying father as addressing his son Judas בני יהודה
הנקרא שמך מכבי על גבורתך, *my son Judas who art
named Machabee on account of thy bravery.*[1]) But it
does not appear whether he derives this from a Hebrew root, or from what he knows of Judas' character.
It is certain that some derivations of the ancient wri-
ters have no connection with the Hebrew whatever,
but are simply the conjectures of those who did not
wish to seem ignorant of the name[2]).

Such is the suggestion of Nicolas de Lyra[3]) that

---

1) See Lib. III. Cap. IX. Comp. 1 Machab. II, 66 and Josephus
Antiq. XII, 6, 3.

2) Azaria de Rossi, who belongs to the first half of the sixteenth century, adopts the opinion of a certain Samotheus (John Lucidus) in lib. II. c. X of his *"Emendationes temporum"* (Venet. 1546),
that Machabeus is a Greek word and that its signification in the
Italian is Paladino: לדברי סמוט"ראו ספר ב' פר' ר' מכב"ראי היא יונית ופתרונה
באיטלקי פאלדי"ני: See Meor Enajim f. 142ᵇ ed. Vienna.

3) *Interpretatio autem Machabai protegens vel protectio, et
de ipso dicitur 1 Machab. III, 3 Et protegebat castra gladio suo.*
Pars quarta f. 428ᵃ, ed. MDVII.

the name means *"protegens vel protectio"*, It is evident
that he is not thinking of any Hebrew word, for what
could he mean? but rather what seemed to him the
chief characteristic of Judas as contained in the pane-
gyric 1 Machabees III, 1—9.
A similar theory was mentioned by Zipser in the
Jewish journal Ben Chananja for Oct. 1. 1860, according to which Matthias and his five sons were called
מחובאים the concealed, because they sought conceal-
ment from the wrath of Antiochus. In support of this
theory he refers to 1 Sam. XXIII, 23, where Saul char-
ges the Ziphites to become acquainted with all David's
hiding places (מְכֹּל הַמַּחֲבֹאִים). But such a derivation
would furnish no special designation for Judas above
the rest of the family, to say nothing of the utter improbability of such an etymology.

An onomasticon at the end of a Latin MS. of the
Vulgate[1]), which probably belongs to the thirteenth
century, interprets the meaning of Machabeus as *"protegens aut protectio sive percutiens aut ingeniosus"*. The
word *percutiens* might be connected with the root כאב
to grieve, from which the Hiphil participle occurs,
which signifies *to cause grief*, and which is said of
their enemies when the prophet prophesies that "there
shall be no more a pricking brier unto the house of
Israel nor any *piercing* thorn of all that are about
them who despised them".[2]) Machabeus might signify
one who is a thorn in the sides of the enemy, but
the form of the name is against it. The contraction
is allowable, but it is improbable that מכאבי would be
written instead of מכאיבי.

---

1) This MS. is in the library of Dr. J. H. R. Biesenthal.
2) Ezechiel XXVIII, 24.

In the onomasticon of a Latin MS. belonging to the sixteenth century the name is given *Machabeus*, *pugnator*,[1]) but a word from which the name could be derived with this signification does not exist, besides such a designation would be a mere truism.

In much the same way Isidor of Pelusium says that Machabee is to be interpreted just as *Koiranos* among the Persians i. e. Despot. Μαχχαβαῖος γὰρ ἑρμη- νεύεται, οἱονεὶ παρὰ Πέρσαις, κοίρανος, τουτέστι δεσπότης. Epist. III, 4. But I do not know of any Persian word of a corresponding form which has this signification, moreover the Machabean age had no connection with Persia.

Filosseno Luzzatto's[2]) conjecture that the name is an inversion of βιαιομάχας a valiant warrior, to say nothing of the improbability of such an artificial trans- position as he suggests, is condemned by the fact that Mattathias and all his followers entertained a bitter hatred for every thing that was Grecian.

The next group of theories which I shall consider may be termed *Abbrevial*, i. e. each letter in the name is supposed to be the initial or final letter of a word.[3]) If the name is composed of initials it is termed rabbinically ר״ה i. e. רָאשֵׁי תֵּיבוֹת, but if of final letters it is indicated by ס״ת i. e. סוֹפֵי תֵּיבוֹת. Of the

---

1) This MS. is in the Royal library at Berlin.

2) Giudaismo Illustrato di Samuel David Luzzatto, Padova 1848, p. 88. „Mio figlio Filosseno vede nel vocabulo *Maccabeo* una inver- sione del greco *Biaiomachas*, che vale *strenuo pugnatore*, da cui se fece primieramente *Machabiaios*, indi *Machabaios* ed in latino *Machabaeus*.

3) Buxtorf, *de Abbreviaturis*, names the first species inaccura- tely נוֹטָרִיקוֹן. A proper example of the Notaricon is furnished in the analysis of אדם into אפר (dust), דם (blood) and מרה (gall).

above named group there are four which may be considered under two distinct heads: *first* that which derives the name from בׄ קׄ מׄ (סׄ הׄ). The supporters of this
opinion are Reland and the late Rabbi Dr. Zipser,
who both agree as to the origin of these letters with
reference to the name.[1])

According to Numb. II, 9—14 the children of Israel wese gathered into four camps around the stan-
dards of Judah, Reuben, Simeon and Gad. Verse 2 reads:
*Every man of the children of Israel shall pitch by his
own standard, with the ensign of their father's house.*
(אִישׁ עַל־דִּגְלוֹ בְאֹתֹת לְבֵית אֲבֹתָם יַחֲנוּ בְּנֵי יִשְׂרָאֵל:). And Aben
Ezra says: *The ancients say that on the banner of Reuben
there was the figure of a man, on that of Judah a lion.
on that of Ephraim an ox, and on that of Gad an eagle.*[2])

Besides these figures it is said that on these ban-
ners were inscribed the names of the Patriarchs אברם, יצחק
and יעקב. On the standard of Reuben were the letters
אׄ רׄ י, of Judah בׄ צׄ ע, of Ephraim רׄ חׄ ק, and of Gad מׄ קׄ ב.

Reland says that the name Μαχχαβαῖος may have
been derived from the fact that Matthatias dwelt in
Modin,[3]) a village in the territory of Gad, and that
the name may have come from the letters which were
on the banner of Gad.

Zipser's theory is still more finely spun. He su-
poses that after the well known treaty between *Judas*
and the Romans[4]) some pledge of friendliness was demanded from the Jews, and that nothing could be

---

1) Relandi Palestina p. 901 (*Modin*). Zipser in Ben-Chananja
den 1ten Oct. 1860, S. 497—504.
2) Comp. the Targum of Pseudo-Jonathan on Numb. Chap. II.
3) See 1 Machab. II, 1, 15; IX, 19.
4) 1 Machab. VIII, 17—32.

more grateful to their allies than the adoption of the Roman eagle, which was rendered possible since it already
existed on the ensign of Dan, and as the letters מ קב
were also embroidered upon the banner Judas received
them as a surname. Neither of these theories, which
rest upon mere fables, is worthy of a moment's consideration. The latter is still further condemned by
the supposition that the pious Judas forsooth would
accept of that abomination a Roman eagle!

The two other initial theories have more in their
favor. The former, mentioned by Prof. Delitzsch in his
Geschichte der jüdischen Poesie, Leipzig 1836, *S.* 28, is
the conjecture of Raphael Fürstenthal that מכ"בּ =
מַתִּתְיָה כֹהֵן בֵּן יוֹדָן.[1]) But a name with such an origin
would no more belong to Judas than to the rest of
the brothers. His name was certainly more distinctive.

The latter theory which was first mentioned by
Azaria de Rossi in *Meôr Enajim* by Rabbi Gedalia ben
Joseph Jachia in *Shalsheleth Hakkabbala*, and which
is indicated by the pointing in some of the MSS. of
the Megillath Antiochos is very attractive and in the
seventeenth century had many adherents. It has been
more recently supported by Oppenheim in Nos. 5, 6
and 43 of the *Maggid* (*Jewish Intelligencer*) for 1873.
This theory supposes that the name has arisen from
the initials of the words מִי כָּמוֹכָה בָּאֵלִים יְהֹוָה (Ex. XV. 11.)
Who is like unto thee o Lord among the Gods? It
was supposed that these initials were stitched upon
the banner of Judas, as S.P.Q.R on those of the Romans, and that he afterwards received his name from

---

[1]) Dr. J. H. R. Biesenthal holds that this is the only probable
derivation. It is also adopted by Baer Frank in his edition of the
מגלת אנטיובוס 1860.

these letters. I think that this theory is worthy of a
special examination. It is not necessary to suppose
that these letters were stitched on a banner. They
could have been used as a battle cry. I do not know
of any example in the Bible which illustrates this initial theory. There are names which are composed of a
sentence: יוֹשֵׁב חֶסֶד *Mercy is requited;* טוֹב אֲדוֹנָיָהוּ *Good is
my Lord Jahu;* אֶלְיוֹעֵינַי *Towards the Lord are my eyes.*
But there is no name which is composed of initials. The
fact that no analogous case of a name occurs does
not disprove the possibility of such a combination.
To say that such a name is the invention of a cabbalistic[1]) age does not dispose of the theory. Such a
combination might arise at any period. Just as the
figure of a fish on account of its Greek name[2]) became
the emblem of Christ, so the initials of these words
might have been connected with the already existing
name Machabee, which had already originated in
some other way. We know that after Judas had ob-
tained a brilliant victory over Gorgias the people sang
either the 118. or the 136. Psalm (1 Machabees IV,
24—25), and it is quite possible that they sang the
words *Who o Lord is like thee among the Gods?* The
acrostic of this verse might have been recognized and
applied to his name while Judas was yet living, with
reference to his frequent appeals to God as the one
who would vindicate the cause of his people.[3])

1) The following are fair specimens of cabbalistic ingenuity:
אַיָל = אֱלֹהִים יִרְאֶה־לּוֹ Gen. XXII, 8. 13 and the cabbalistic name of God
Agla אגלא = אַתָּה גִּבּוֹר לְעוֹלָם אֲדֹנָי. Both of these examples are instances of Râshê Thêboth.

2) IXΘΥΣ stood for Ἰησοῦς Χριστὸς Θεοῦ Υἱὸς Σωτήρ.

3) Oppenheim urges in favor of the formation of the name
from מִי כָמֹכָה בָּאֵלִים יהוה, that already in the Machabean period

3

I now come to the *hammer* theory which is based
on the reading מקבי. I shall briefly consider *its origin,
its claims, and the reason for its rejection.*

1. *Origin of this theory.*

The first to defend the reading מקבי was *Conrad Iken* († 1735) on the ground of the Syriac (ܡܩܒܐ)
and Arabic (مقبى) transcriptions of the name. He
mentions incidentally that מַקָּב and מַקָּבָא mean hammer,
and perhaps thus far prepares the way for *J. D. Michaelis.* In support of his theory he appeals to the explanations of the name by Isidor of Pelusium, Jusippon
ben Gurion, Azaria de Rossi, John Lucidus, Rabbi
David Gans[1]) and others. He does not however ex-
plain the word as a figurative appellative of Judas as
a hero, but starts from the general signification of
thrusting through.[2]) No doubt he is aiming at the

abbreviations were in use, e. g. on the coins of Simon brother of
Judas there are the following: שב for שנת ב', שג for שנת ג' and שד
for שנת ד'. Compare Madden, *History of Jewish coinage* p. 43—45.
I can add as another illustration that, according to the Mishna,
in the times of persecution a single letter was put on vessels as the
initial of a word: ק = קרבן, מ = מעשר, ד = דמאי, ט = טבל, ח = תרומה.
See *Maäser* IV, 11. Comp. the mason's marks, of which an account
is given in the *Palestine Exploration Fund* 1870 p. 324. All these
examples however furnish no particular support for the theory.

1) This historian († 1613) says, although ignorant of Greek,
והוא נקרא יהודה מכבאי ע"ש גבורתי כי מכבא בלשון יון גבור ואיש מלחמה *And
he is called Judas Machabeus on account of his bravery, since ma-
chaba in the Greek language signifies brave and warlike.* Zemach
David f. 21[5].

2) "Non enim solum كَبَّ, unde supra vidimus regulariter
vocem מַקָּב derivari, apud Arabes inter alia denotat *invasit, adflixit,
prostravit,* quod ipsum fortitudinis, roboris, virtutisque bellicae opus
est, sed et propius adhuc convenit radix נקב per ק, unde commo-
dissime Graecum Μαχχαβαῖος per χ scriptum deduci monuimus; apud
Hebraeos enim Chaldaeos, Syros, ut et Samaritanos atque Arabes

right idea, but he loses his way because he accepts the writing with *koph*. Besides there seems to me to be no critical value whatever in the authorities quoted. So far as our lexicons are reliable, there is no foundation at all for the supposition that Machabee is derived from the Greek, Syriac, or Persian. While *Iken's* citations are of interest they must be used with great caution and can have no weight in deciding the question. *Kennicott* († 1783) adopts the reading מקבי because he found it in two MSS. of the Megillath Antiochos in the Bodleian Library, and because it was confirmed by the Syrian.[1]) Yet he does not offer any opinion

proprie denotat *fixit, fodit, perfodit, perforavit,* et نَكَبَ *invasit eum aerumna,* et מַקָּב atque מַקָּבָא Chald. *malleum* et quidem, ut addit Castellus, sigillatim *una parte acutum et ad perforandum aptum, altera ad percutiendum,* conf. Arabum مِنقَب; quae omnia quam egregie iterum ad robur, virtutemque bellicam quadrent, nemo non videt, unde et similes locutiones in omnibus linguis ad fortitudinem in bello transferri et inprimis etiamnum qui in haereticis (liceat voce sensu in scholis theologorum recepto uti) profligandis eorumque vi retundenda prae aliis strenuus est, malleus haereticorum appellari consuevit. Quid quod ipsum nomen مَقْبَة quod Hebraei scriberent מַקָּבָה *makkaba* aut Syri ܡܰܩܰܒܐ Arabibus *Virtutem et rem qua quis gloriari possit* denotat." Conrad Iken, Symbolae Literariae etc. Tom. I p. 192—93.

1) "Unicum tantum in hoc loco sigillatim ex eo adduxisse juvabit, utrumque nimirum hoc MS. nos adjuvare in detegendo errore aliquo a Buxtorfio, Pridosio et omnibus fere viris doctis in inepta vocis *Maccabaeorum* derivatione commisso. Haec etenim ex eorum sententia ex quatuor vocum מי כמכה באלים יהוה (Ex. XV, 2) litteris initialibus, quas ipsas Judae Maccabaei vexillis inscriptas fuisse contendunt, conflata est. Sed cum nomen hoc in utroque MS. scriptum sit מקבי, non מכבי, corruere funditus haec videtur derivatio, inprimis cum MSS. horum lectio Syriaca impressa historiae Maccabaeorum versione confirmetur, quae ubivis hoc nomen per ק exprimit." Kennicotti Dissertatio Secunda, Lipsiae MDCCXV, p. 521—22.

as to its meaning. *J. D. Michaelis* († 1791) having accepted Kennicotts reading was the author of the hammer theory in nearly its present form.[1]) He says that the name is written מקבי, that it comes from the word מקבת, a hammer, and that those who gave Judas the name compared him on account of his valiant deeds in war with a hammer, which dashes the enemy in pieces and which is used in hammering iron. He further suggests that the image might have been borrowed from Zachar. II, 3—4, in which passage the word חרשים was very likely understood as referring to blacksmiths, which is the common interpretation.

The only new elements which this theory has received from its numerous supporters, among whom are Gesenius, Ewald, Grimm and Keil, is the comparison with Charles Martel, and the assertion that double kappa indicates a *koph.*[2])

2. *Claims of this theory.*

I must admit that the Biblical imagery is favorable to it although the passage already cited Zach. II,

---

1) Der Name wird Hebräisch מקבי geschrieben, wie man aus der syrischen Uebersetzung (ܡܩܒܝ) und dem hebräischen und chaldäischen Buch der Maccabäer, das die Juden haben, siehet. Dies kommt von מקבת, ein Hammer, her: diejenigen die ihm den Namen gaben, verglichen ihn wegen seiner grossen Thaten im Kriege mit einem Hammer, der die Feinde zerschmetterte und auch Eisen hämmerte. Vielleicht borgten sie das Bild aus Zachar. II, 3. 4 und verstanden dort חרשים, wie man gemeiniglich thut, von Schmieden. ... Kennicotts zweite Dissertation über den gedruckten hebräischen Text hat mir zuerst den gewöhnlichen Irrthum benommen, und die Vergleichung der syrischen Uebersetzung hat mich noch mehr gewiss gemacht." J. D. Michaelis deutsche Uebersetzung des ersten Buchs der Maccabäer mit Anmerkungen. Göttingen und Leipzig 1778, S. 48.

2) Vaihinger, Herzog's Real-Encycl. B. 8. S. 737.

3—4 can hardly serve the purpose of those who use it. It is true that הָרָשִׁים [1]) is equivalent to חָרָשֵׁי בַרְזֶל (blacksmiths), but the comparison of princes with smiths in this passage is simply, because those princes who have scattered Israel to the four winds are likened to horns, and the completion of the figure demands that the instruments of the divine punishment which cut them off should be compared with smiths.

Nevertheless the figure of dashing in pieces is used several times in the Old Testament to represent a conqueror. 1) מֵפִיץ from פָּץ to dash in pieces, of a vessel, Psalm II, 9; to scatter, of a people Jer. XIII, 14. It occurs in Jer. LI, 20: *Thou art my battle a.re and weapons of war: for with thee will I break in pieces the nations.*[2]) 2) מֵפִיץ from פוּץ to break in pieces; to scatter, used in Nahum II, 2, of a warrior, *A disperser is come up against thee.*[3]) 3) The onomatopoetic word פַּטִּישׁ[4]) *hammer, sledge,* is mentioned as a smith's hammer, Is. XLI, 7; a sledge with which rocks are broken, Jer. XXIII, 29; and is used figuratively of Babylon as the great conquering power, Jer. L, 23: *How is*

---

1) The Targum renders this word by אוּמָנִים *Artificer.* Rashi says in loco: נַגָּרִים הֵיוֹדְעִים לְנַסֵּר אֶת הַקְרָנִית וּרְבוֹתֵינוּ פֵּירְשׁוּ בְּמַסֶּכֶת סוּכָּה מִי הֵם: *(The word signifies) workmen who know how to cut (off) the horns, and our Rabbies have explained in the treatise Succa (52ᵇ) who they are.*

2) מַפֵּץ־אַתָּה לִי כְּלֵי מִלְחָמָה וְנִפַּצְתִּי בְךָ גּוֹיִם וְהִשְׁחַתִּי בְךָ מַמְלָכוֹת:

3) עָלָה מֵפִיץ עַל־פָּנָיִךְ The translation of the English version, *he that dasheth in pieces,* is not favored by the use of the language. הֵפִיץ is one of the synonymic terms for the dispersion of Israel.

4) Comp. فِطِّيس which has been adopted by the Arabs to represent a large blacksmith's hammer; the root is the same as of πα-τάσσω, *batuo,* French *battre,* Eng. *bat,* and vulgar German *patschen.*

the hammer of the whole earth cut off and broken in pieces. [1]) This word is also in common use in Aramaic and the Rabbinical Hebrew. [2])

3. *Reasons for the rejection of the Hammer theory.*

Hence although the comparison of Judas with a sledge hammer which breaks rocks in pieces would be perfectly in keeping with the imagery of the above passages, yet the reading מִקֵּב is without sufficient foundation as has already been shown.

Besides considering the use of the words מַקָּב מַקֶּבֶת, מַקָּבָה (Aramaic מַקָּב or מִקּוּב) I find that the so-called instrument was of medium size such as Jael could easily wield with one hand, Jud. IV, 21; and that it was used for finishing the edges of stone 1 K. VI, 7. It was the smaller blacksmith's hammer, which was used in fashioning iron for the idol Is. XLIV, 12; and for driving nails to fasten it in its place Jer. X. 4. Now when we remember the comparative richness of the Hebrew in expressions for hammer [3]) and the tendency of the people to use a concrete term for a name, it is not likely that they would chose מַקָּב as a designation for the dashing bravery of Judas.

I now insert a theory which has been suggested by my revered friend and teacher in the following letter.

---

1) אֵיךְ נִגְדַּע וַיִּשָּׁבֵר פַּטִּישׁ כָּל־הָאָרֶץ

2) In Jer. L, 23 the Targum renders פַּטִּישׁ by מַלְכָּא דַּהֲוָה מְזִיחַ לְכָל־אַרְעָא *(The king who was shaking the entire earth).* In Berachoth 28[b] the dying Rabban Jochanan ben Zaccai is addressed by his disciples: נר ישראל עמוד הימיני פטיש החזק *O light of Israel, right hand pillar, strong hammer!*

3) The Hebrew has six different designations for hammer, the Chaldee seven, and the Arabic nineteen (at least according to Freytag's Lexicon).

Leipzig, 22. November 1875.

To the Rev. Samuel Ives Curtiss, Jr.

Dear Sir:

I said to you lately that I too had wrought out a theory of my own about the name Maccabee. As you desired to know what it was, I now write it, so that you may have it in black and white.

For my part, I start from the supposition that the name מכבי, whose pointing, to judge by the Greek and Latin way of writing it, should be מַכַּבָּי stands in close connection with the Bible names מַכְבַּנַּי 1 Chron. XII, 13 and מַכְנַדְבַי Ezra X, 40, and that these three names should be explained together. No verb beginning with מכ offers itself for the solution of any of the three. Hence it seems to me that the first part of the compound word is the interrogative מַה, used as מִי is in the other compounds, as מִיכָאֵל who is that which God is? מִיכָאֵל who is like God? מִיכָיָהוּ who is like Jahu?

From this as a point of departure

1. The name מַכַּבָּי is explained as an abbreviation of מַה כְּאָבִי what is like (comparable to) my father? The name was not the one given to Judas just after his birth, but a surname added later. It fits the youthful hero exactly. Proud of his father and treading in his footsteps he led to victory the things for which that father had struggled. The contraction is phonetically regular. Compare מֵידָה, מַצַּבְכֶם and מַתְלָאָה Malachi I, 13. The י of the ending was originally a possessive suffix, as also probably in the name הַצְלֶלְפּוֹנִי Give shade thou who turnest towards me, 1 Chron. IV, 3. In the use of the name however, it came to coincide with the י ־. of the relative adjective (the "Nisba" as the Arabs call it) since the name designates one who boasts of his father as an incomparable man.

2. The name מַכְבַּנַּי, analogously with the foregoing, means, "What is like (comparable to) my children?", as is suggested dubiously in Gesenius' Lexicon. It should indeed really be מַכְבְּנַי or מִכְבָּנַי, but the dagesh thrown to the end of the word is due to the fact that the name was thus made easier to pronounce. The intensifying of the Nun is besides

explained by analogy with קְטַנִּים, מְעַדָּנִּים, מִשְׁמַנִּים, and the like.
The dagesh of the nasal is in all these cases euphonic. The
name is easily accounted for as the joyful outcry of the father
at the birth of a healthy and lovely child.

3. The name מַכְבַּדָי explains itself at once after the above.
It means, *What is like (comparable to) my benefactors, or like
my generous friends?* *"The noble"* is נָדָב after the form רָחָב.
The form נְדָבָי, the taking of which as plural is favored by the
aspirated ב, is abbreviated from כְדָבָי. Compare besides the
arabic adjective رَحْب, which corresponds to the Hebrew רָחָב.
A father, seeing himself at the birth of his son surrounded
by a crowd of sympathizing and generous friends, might well
name him thus in honor of these friends. As to the ending י ָ
the same holds good that we remarked above for י .. Originally a possessive pronoun, it has in the later consciousness
of the language lost that sense. All three names are at first,
like הֶפְצִי־בָהּ, words of joyful confession stamped upon the re-
spective persons to characterize them.

Perhaps, my dear friend, you may find these conjectures
not unworthy of being added to the material, which you have
gathered with such zealous research. May you succeed in
throwing light upon the darkness enshrouding this name, so
glorious in the annals of the Jewish nation, and in thrusting
aside the false traditions which one after another of the later
students has copied from his predecessors.

Franz Delitzsch.

I can but feel that this dissertation is only a poor
setting for the communication of so eminent a scholar,
unless it be by the way of contrast. The above explanation is remarkable for its novelty, admirable for
the symmetry and beauty of its statement, and im-
pregnable from an etymological point of view. Yet
while it commends itself in all these particulars and
is strengthened by the analogy of two proper names,
the sense which the explanation gives to the surname

is without support. History suggests and tradition demands for מכבי a signification which in some way indicates Judas' preeminence as a military leader.[1]

III.

As has already been indicated *Machabeus* is a cognomen or surname. In determining its signification it must be remembered 1) that names of this class are seldom if ever given at birth[2]; 2) that they often either memorialize some important event in the persons history, indicate some distinguishing trait in his character, or give some hint of his life work. Compare *Israel*, Gen. XXXII, 28; *Boanerges, sons of thunder*, Mark III, 17; and *Barnabas, son of consolation*, Acts IV, 36.

In order that we may determine what appellative might fittingly be given to Judas let us briefly glance at the history of that period. The condition of the

---

1) Comp. 1 Machab. II, 66 "Καὶ Ἰούδας Μακκαβαῖος ἰσχυρὸς δυνάμει ἐκ νεότητος αὐτοῦ, οὗτος ὑμῖν ἔσται ἄρχων στρατιᾶς καὶ πολεμήσει πόλεμον λαῶν." III, 1 "Καὶ ἀνέστη Ἰούδας ὁ καλούμενος Μακκαβαῖος." Josephus Antiq. XII, 6, 3 „Μακκαβαῖον δὲ τῆς στρατιᾶς, δι᾽ ἀνδρείαν καὶ ἰσχὺν, στρατηγὸν ἔξητε." A passage cited by Reland from an Etymologicon is worthy of notice in this connection: "Τῇ δὲ Σύρῳ διαλέκτῳ ἀνδρεῖος, πολεμιστὴς δυνατώτατος." Dissertationum Miscell. Pars II (Trajecti ad Rhenum MDCCVII) p. 188. The Aramaic idiom which was spoken in Palestine was called Syriac.

2) The name Βαρσαβᾶς, Acts I, 23, can be regarded as an exception. According to Dr. Biesenthal, who is remarkable for his knowledge of the Talmud and Jewish customs, Βαρσαβᾶς is equivalent to בַּר שַׁבְּתָא a name which was given to every son who was born on the Sabbath. It was hoped that such a person would be preeminently pious, hence Joseph Barsabas received the further surname Ἰοῦστος, because such a man was called קַדִּישׁ. See *Shabbath* 165ᵃ.

4

Jews in the time of Mattathias[1]) was most pitiable. An insolent blasphemous and cruel foe filled the land, desecrated their sacred places, profaned their holy books, prohibited the rite of circumcision, and demanded the absolute renunciation of their religious observances. In such times new energies, new ideas and new words are evoked, and popular leaders are measured and named with reference to their fitness for the demands of the age. The one thought of Mattathias and his followers might well have been: How shall we *extinguish* these firebrands which are spreading death and desolation throughout the land, who shall be our leader in this great work? The passage which I have already quoted, 1 Machabees II, 66 indicates that Judas had exhibited martial qualities which led to his selection as commander. Certainly it is not improbable that the hopes which his youthful daring inspired should be expressed in a name which future events might, to a certain extent, render prophetic.

Now regarding מכבי as a simple word there is but one probable, I might almost say possible, derivation for it, and that is from כָּבָה *to be extinguished*, Piel *to extinguish*. This verb occurs in the Old Testament twenty three times and is used of the *extinction* 1) *of a fire or a lamp* Lev. VI, 5. 1 Sam. III, 3; 2) *of God's wrath* 2 Kings XXII, 17; 3) *of human life* 2 Samuel XIV, 7, XXI, 17; 4) *of love* Canticles VIII, 7; 5) *of an army*, Isaiah XLIII, 17 *which bringeth forth the*

1) His name is written, wherever it occurs in the Old Testament, מַתִּתְיָה or מַתִּתְיָהוּ, hence the punctuation מַתִּתְיָה in Gesenius' Lexicon deviates from the masoretic pointing. The Greek form of the name Ματταθίας probably indicates the original pronunciation of the word, the later form of the name having arisen through the weakening of *a* to *i*.

27

*chariot and horse, the army and the power; they shall lie
down together they shall not rise: they are extinct, they are
quenched as tow.*[1]) God threatens four different times
by the mouth of his prophets Isaiah I, 31; Jeremiah
IV, 4, XXI, 12; Amos V, 6 to kindle a fire which
none shall be able to quench (אֵין מְכַבֶּה). It is not
necessary that I should determine the nature of this
fire, the terrible part of the prophecy is that there
shall be no extinguisher.

As the pious Jew in the time of Antiochus re-
flected upon the apostacy of many of his countrymen
and their miserable condition, would it be strange if
he remembered these prophecies, and compared the
hostile armies to the fire which God had kindled in
punishment of sin, and as in the mournful age of the
captivity one of the Jews bore the name חֲרַחְיָה, "*wrath
of Jah*" Neh. III, 8, so now the hope might be expressed that as God had extinguished the Egyptians
in the Red sea, he would again have compassion on

---

1) הַמּוֹצִיא רֶכֶב־וָסוּס חַיִל וְעִזּוּז יַחְדָּו יִשְׁכְּבוּ בַּל־יָקוּמוּ דָּעֲכוּ כַּפִּשְׁתָּה כָבוּ:
Compare Koran V, 69 كُلَّمَا أَوْقَدُوا نَارًا لِلْحَرْبِ أَطْفَأَهَا ٱللَّهُ *As
often as they kindled a fire for the war Allah extinguished it.*
أَخْبَى ٱلْحَرْبَ *He extinguished (the fire of) the war.* See Lane's
Lexicon. War is often compared to fire. Numbers XXI, 28, 30
(Prof. Delitzsch remarks that very likely the last clause of the 30th
verse should be read בְּהִנָּשֵׂא אֵשׁ *during the blowing up of the fire
[of war]*), and Ps. LXXVIII, 63. The exciter of a war is termed
in Arabic مِغْسَرُ ٱلْحَرْبِ i. e. the stick with which one stirs up a
fire (Gesenius, Thesaurus I. p. 157 b), compare Barhebracus' description
of a massacre at Edessa: ܕܠܚ ܘܐܝܟ ܢܘܪܐ ܒܩܣܐ ܗܟܢܐ ܢܘܪܐ ܕܛܝܝܐ
*As the fire in the stubble so, the fire of the Turks prevailed among
them.* See Barhebraei Chron. Syr. p. 333, and Gesenius Commen-
tar über Jesaia, 2. Theil. S. 381.

4*

his people and raise up a Machabee (מכבה) in the person of Judas — a hope which was gloriously realized in his subsequent career.

With reference to the form, I must allow that מכבי can only be derived from the Hiphil. While it is true that Biblical usage might lead us to expect the already existing Piel, it cannot be proved that the Hiphil was not in use among the people.[1]

In several verbs there is scarcely any perceptible difference in the signification of the Piel and Hiphil, both being used side by side to give a transitive meaning where the Kal is intransitive, as in the case before us e. g. אִבַּד and הֶאֱבִיד to utterly destroy; מוֹתֵת and הֵמִית to put to death;[2] hence מְכַבֶּה[3]) as well as מְכַבֶּה can signify one who extinguishes, and מְכַבִּי the extinguisher[4]. But some one may ask whether the termination י - would not indicate a descendant from מְכַבֶּה as מְנַשִּׁי signifies a descendant of מְנַשֶּׁה. I reply: not

_____

1) We often meet in proper names forms of the verbs, which the use of the language does not otherwise recognize, e. g. רַחַבְיָה Jah makes wide, where the Kal has the signification of the Hiphil; מַלַּטְיָה Jah delivers, where the Kal is used in the signification of the Piel and Hiphil (once, Is. XXXI, 5). See Köhler, Sacharja I S. 3.

2) Ewald, Lehrbuch der hebr. Sprache, Göttingen 1870, S. 315. Comp. Wright's Arabic Grammar, London 1874. §. 45. Rem. a.

3) The second a in Machabeus does not conflict with the derivation from the Hiphil, since it probably first entered in the transscription; compare הַמְדָתָא Amadathi, מְכַבַּי Μαχαβανί, צַרְקִי Aracaeus &c.

4) It is evident that the Greek translator considered the termination י . or more properly י - as a nisba, otherwise he would have written the word Μαχαβί or Μαχαβαί like אֲבִי Ἀβί, שַׁבְתַי Σαββαθαί, but he has followed the analogy of patronymics, gentiles &c. e. g. אַנְגִי ἀγαῖος, אֱמֹרִי ἀμορραῖος, קֵנִי κενεζαῖος.

necessarily, since in this case it indicates one who ex-
hibits the properties of an extinguisher as זְבְרִי is one
who manifests the characteristics of the זָבָּר or זְבָּר i. e.
foreigner; רַגְלִי a footman, compare the Aramaic סַקַּן
the sack-maker.[1])

I grant that this derivation is a conjecture. Absolute certainty with our present sources of information is impossible.

I claim however as the result of impartial investigation that this theory which I have twice rejected
has at last after a careful examination the greatest
weight not only on account of its correspondence
with the probable reading, but also because it is so
completely in harmony with Semitic imagery, represents
so clearly the great problem of the age, the extinction
of the enemy, and so truly indicates the character of
Judas as a victorious general.

The difficulties which attend such an investigation
can only be fully realized by experience. I trust that
these materials may render subsequent investigations
in this line less difficult, and prove of assistance in
shedding more light upon one of the most interesting
pages of Jewish history. It must however be confes-
sed that until we discover the same sources that Jerome and Origen possessed, no investigator can abso-
lutely determine the etymology of the name or its
signification.

<hr />

1) See Geiger Lehr- und Lesebuch zur Sprache der Mischna
Abtheil. 1, Breslau 1845, S. 48. Moreover the following Biblical
proper names, whose י. does not seem to be patronymical, are
worthy of comparison: גְּמַלִּי, בַּרְמִי, מַחְלִי, שׁוֹבִי, שְׁלוֹמִי; especially נַפְתָּלִי
which is an example of a *nisba* formed from a Niphal participle,
compare Ewald § 156°.

Appendix I.

Σαρβήθ Σαρβανιέλ. The following translations have been proposed: 1) שרביט סרבני אל *The rod of those who rebel against God*. Herzfeld, Geschichte des Volkes Jisrael. Band II, S. 457.

2) שרביט שר בני אל *The government* (properly the sceptre) *of the prince of God's sons*. Ewald, Geschichte des Volkes Israel, Göttingen 1864 IV, 604 Anmerk. 1.

3) סרבת סרבני אל *The obstinacy of those who resist God*. Geiger, Urschrift S. 205 unten.

4) ספר בית שר בני אל *Book of the house of the prince of God's children*. Derenbourg, Palestine, p. 451.

5) שרבת שרי בני אל *History of the princes of God's children*". Jahn, Einleitung in die apokryphischen Schriften des A. T., Grimm and others. A comparison of these different readings with the Greek shows that they all vary more or less from it. Number 5 so far as the sense is concerned is the most natural. The word שָׁרְבַּת however does not occur in Hebrew or Chaldee, but is a Syriac word ܫܰܪܒܬܐ which is not directly equivalent to the masculine ܫܰܪܒܐ *history, narration*, but signifies rather *generation, race, family, tribe, people*. The title of the book may be similar to the old Hebrew תולדות, which signifies genealogy, and in a wider range history.

Appendix II.

Examples of the transcription of proper names by the Alexandrian translators and Jerome.

אֶבֶן בֹּהַן λίθον Βαιών *Abenboen* Josh. XVIII, 17.

אֲבִינָדָב 'Αμιναδάβ *Abinadab* 1 Sam. XVI, 8.

אֲבִיהוּא 'Αβιούδ *Abiu* Ex. 6, 23.

אַבְשָׁלוֹם ’Aβεσσαλώμ *Absalom* 2 Chron. XI, 20.

עֲקָן ’Ιουκάμ *Acan* Gen. XXXVI, 28.

אַדְבְּאֵל Ναβδεήλ *Adbeel* Gen. 25, 13.

There are a multitude of examples which show that, while the LXX have transposed and metamorphosed, headed and beheaded ad libitum, Jerome has transcribed the names accurately. Compare Joshua XV, 22—63, of which I give for convenience the first two verses:

קַבְצְאֵל וְעֵדֶר וְיָגוּר: καὶ Βαισελεήλ καὶ ’Aρὰ καὶ ’Aσώρ,

וְקִינָה וְדִימוֹנָה וְעַדְעָדָה: καὶ ’Ικάμ καὶ ’Pεγμὰ καὶ ’Aρουήλ,

וְקֶדֶשׁ וְחָצוֹר וְיִתְנָן: καὶ Κάδης καὶ ’Aσοριωναὶν καὶ Μαινάμ

זִיף וָטֶלֶם וּבְעָלוֹת: καὶ Βαλμαιναὶν καὶ αἱ κῶμαι αὐτῶν.

Cabseel et Eder et Jagur,
et Cina et Dimona et Adada,
et Cades, et Asor, et Jethnam,
Ziph et Telem et Baloth.

Appendix III.

Although the Rabbinical transcription of Greek and Latin words, as exhibited by *Simon* and *Mardochai Bondi*,[1]) is not so exact as that of Jerome, yet it confirms the position that the form *Machabeus* renders an original מקבי highly improbable.

There are fourteen words in which *chi* and *ch* are rulably transcribed with *kaph* and thirteen in which *kappa* and *c* are given with the same letter as follows:

---

1) See אור אסתר Beleuchtung der im Talmud von Babylon und Jerusalem, in Targumim und Midraschim vorkommenden fremden, besonders lateinischen Wörter. Dessau 1812.

Scala אסכלה; κύπη *cupa* כובא; κολεός *culleus* כולייא;
cucullus כבלא; *clavus* כלבוס; κάψα *capsa* כפשה; Καρχηδό-
νιοι Carchedonii כרכדניא; λόγχη *lancea* לונכי; *lacca* לכא;
στάκτη *stacte* סטכת; περισκελίς *periscelis* פרסכלה; *carruca*
קרוכין; καθολικός *catholicus* קתלכוס.

In one hundred and thirty nine words *c* is rendered with *koph*. There are only four in which *koph* is
used for the transcription of *chi* or *ch* e. g. χάλυψ *cha-
lybs* קלוב, χάρτης *charta* קרטס (and כרטס), *sampsuchum*
טמשוק, *chalcanthum* קלקנתום.

If then Jerome never renders *koph* in the Old
Testament with *ch* exept in two cases which may be
accounted for by the presence of *cheth*, if the Rabbins
very rarely transcribe *ch* with *koph*, while there are
are many cases in which *c* is given through *kaph* not
only by them but also in the Old Testament, we have
the strongest presumptive evidence in the reading
Machabeus, that מכבי was the original form.

Appendix IV. [1]

The Hebrew discriminates between the endings
aj and *åj*, even in such cases where they are unquestion-
bly nisbas, as follows:

I. All proper names ending in *aj* are written in
the Old Testament with *pathach*:

מְהָרַי 2 Sam. XXIII, 28 and 1 Chron. XI, 30; סִבְּכַי
XI, 29; אִתַּי בֶּן־רִיבַי XI, 31; חוּרַי XI, 32; עֵרִי XI, 37;
עֲמָשַׂי XII, 18; אֶלְעוּזַי XII, 5; יִשַׁי Ruth IV, 22 and often,
compare אִישַׁי = יִשַׁי 1 Chron. II, 13. For the interchange
of *ji* and *'i* compare Wellhausen, Text der Bücher Sa-
muelis, Seite V f.

II. The Pathach of such proper names becomes
Kamets only in pausa:
יִשָׁי 1 Chron. II, 12. Ruth IV, 22. אֶזְרָי 1 Chron.
XI, 37; אַחְלָי XI, 41. כָּלָי Neh. XI, 8. צוּרִישַׁדָּי Numb. I, 6;
עַמִּישַׁדָּי I, 12.

III. All those proper names, which in unpointed
text are written אי—, must be read with the ending
aj, e. g. שָׁמַאי[1], read שַׁמַּי 1 Chron. II, 28; מִרְאָי[2], read
מִרְאִי; hence מִכְבַּאי, read מִכְבַּי.

IV. In Syriac all such proper names are written
with *Petâchâ* e. g. ‏ܙܰܝ‎ = זַי; ‏ܡܰܝ‎ = מַי; hence according
to the rule ‏ܡܰܟܒܰܝ‎[3] (compare Assemani Bibliotheca Orientalis, Tom. I, p. 72, Tom. III, Pars II p. 346) = מִכְבַּי.

V. In every place where the reading *aj* occurs in
appellative nouns, patronymics, gentiles, and others the

---

1) The right pronunciation of שָׁמַאי ינאי, זכאי has been given
by Zalman Henau in his Siddur שערי תפלה 1725. The author of the
masoretic treatise סדר אברהם Frankfurt on the Oder, 1752 (Catalogue of Lotze's Library No. 194) wrongly makes the objection that
the Biblical שַׁמַּי is not the same name as the Talmudic שמאי.

2) The form מכבאי occurs in Breithaupt's Josephus Hebraicus,
Buxtorf's de Abbreviaturis p. 132 and elsewhere. My own MS. of
Jusippon has מכבי (fol. 11ᵃ etc.).

3) R. Payne Smith, Dean of Canterbury, author of an admirable
Syriac lexicon, of which three fasciculi have appeared, very truly
writes: There is no doubt that the right spelling (of this name) is
‏ܡܰܟܒܰܝ‎. Other forms are ‏ܡܰܟܒܰܝ‎ Ephraem Syri Opera Tom. II. Ro-
mae 1740 p. 312, and ‏ܡܟܒܝ‎ Waltoni Biblia Polyglotta Tom. IV.

Syriac has *Zekafâ* and the Biblical Chaldee *Kamets* e. g.
כְּשׁוֹדִי Chaldean, קַדְמָי *first;* זַכָּי (זַכַּי) *innocent.* On the
contrary when such nouns occur in the Talmud it is
customary to read *Pathach* instead of *Kamets* e. g.
יְהוֹדִי = יְהוּדִי; וַדַּאי = וַדַּי *veritable;* תַּנָּאי = תַּנָּי *teacher*
of the Mishna, or תְּנַי *condition.*

Appendix Vᵃ.

The two Ethiopic transcriptions of the name
Machabee መቃብስ: *Makâbîs* and መካቤው: *Makbêjû* have
arisen in the same way as the two transcriptions in
the different MSS. of the Megillath Antiochos. While
they do not furnish any data for the true reading of
the name, the former points unerringly to the Greek
Μαχαβαῖος (Μακκαβαῖος), the latter to the Latin *Macha-*
beus. That either transcription has an immediate or
even a remote connection with the original Hebrew is
most unlikely. The Abyssinian Bible is a translation
from the Alexandrian version. [1] Although the Ethiopic
translation of the books of the Machabees, from
the Greek, if ever made, has been lost [2], the name

---

1) See Ludolfi Historia Aethiopica, lib. III. cap. 4, and Dillmann
in Herzog's Real-Encyklopädie, Band I, 1854, S. 169.

2) Prof. Dillmann has recently communicated to me the following: „Die Abyssinier besitzen nicht die Maccabäerbücher, welche
sie vielleicht ursprünglich hatten. In meinem Aufsatz in Herzog's
Real-Encyklopädie, sowie in dem Aufsatz *über den Umfang des Bi-*
belcanons der Abyssinischen Kirche in Ewald's Jahrbuch der Biblischen Wissenschaft V (1853) S. 144 ff. nahm ich noch an, dass sie
die Maccabäerbücher haben, weil sie oft genannt werden. Zu Ge-
sicht waren sie mir noch nicht gekommen. Später sah ich Hand-
schriften, worin sie enthalten sein sollten, aber war sehr erstaunt,
zu finden, dass das nicht die biblischen Bücher sind, sondern ein

መቃብ.ስ [1] *Makâbîs* in the fictitious books of the Machabees, which have been fabricated in much the same way as the history of Jusippon ben Gurion, has unquestionably come from the Greek. The form መክቢዩ:[2] *Makbějû*, or መክቢዩስ: *Makbějûs* which is applied to the martyrs of that period and particularly to *Shamuni* (*Samona*), wife of Eleasar and mother of the seven bretheren, occurs in an old poem *Tabîba Tabîbân*[3], and frequently in the Synaxarium[4] (*Legends of the saints*). This form of the name with *Kaf* arose much earlier than the translation of the first and second book of the Machabees from the Vulgate, but it is none the less to he derived either directly or indirectly from the Latin *Machabeus*.

---

elendes, in Abyssinien erdichtetes Machwerk, das sie an die Stelle der verlorenen Bücher schon ziemlich früh gesetzt haben." Compare Dillmann, Lexicon linguae Aethiopicae, Leipzig 1865, Prolegomena, Col. XI.

1) This form of the name occurs in the following MSS. of the Magdala Collection in the British Museum: Oriental 487 f. 131; 489 f. 119ʰ; 491 f. 118ᵇ; 502 f. 169; 504 f. 105ᵇ; 505 f. 39ᵇ; 506 f. 4; in the translation of the first and second of Macchabees from the Vulgate, Orient. 491 f. 168; 504 f. 82; 505 f. 1; and the history of Makâbis Orient. 770, a MS. of the fifteenth century. Comp. *ZDMG.* Band XXIV, S. 599 ff. I have received these details more fully than in the *ZDMG.* through the great kindness of Prof. William Wright, D. D., LL. D. of Cambridge, England.

2) The martyrdom of መክቢዩ: *Makbějû* and her seven sons is in the British Museum, see d'Abbadie No. 179. 34.

3) According to two MSS, the name with *Kaf* occurs in the 76 and 87ᵗʰ stanzas, see Dillmann's Chrestomathia Aethiopica, p. 125; comp. Ludolfi Historia Aethiopica, lib. III. c. 4, §. 20, and Comment. p. 425.

4) I have heard through Prof. Dillmann that the name መክ ሰብ: often occurs in the Synaxarium.

Appendix V^b.

In Syriac the name *Machabee* is only written with *Kôph*. This is due as has already been remarked (p. 9) to the influence of the Greek. It is not probable that the Syrian translator of the first book of Machabees, or Ephraem, in whose works the name is found, ever saw the original Hebrew from which the Greek was translated. Through the rare courtesy of the Dean of Canterbury I am able to give the following passages where the name ܡܟܒܝ occurs in Syriac: *Ephraemi Syri opera omnia*, Tom. secundus, p. 206 line 17 from the bottom; p. 302 line 5; and p. 558 line 7 from the bottom; *Assemani Bibliotheca Orientalis* Tom. II p. 165ª line Syr. 9; Tom. III, pars I. p. 7 line 3; and the references already given; also *Assemani Cat. Bibliothecae Vat.* Tom. II p. 19 lines 7, 11, p. 506 line 11, 507 line 25; Tom. III p. 235 line 3. Dean Smith adds: *"Bar Bahlul* writes ܡܟܒ̈ܝܐ and explains *zealot* ܛܢܢܐ. The shorter form he writes ܡܟܒܝ. *Bar-Ali* in my cod. (*Cod. Hunting. Bibl. Bodleianae*) writes ܛܢܢܐ ܗ ܡܟܒܝܐ. Afterwards ܡܚܡܨ ܗ ܝܬܢܐ الغيور."

Appendix VI.

מגלת אנטיוכס

This book, as Zunz has shown (Gottesdienstliche Vorträge S. 134), is the product of the Middle Ages [1],

---

[1] If we may believe the late Abraham Firkowitsch, Saadja Gaon († 941—2) is the first who in the preface of his work entitled ספר הגלוי cites a verse from the Megillath Antiochos. See the reply of David Oppenheim to Raphael Kirchheim in No. 43 of the Maggid for 1873.

and is utterly destitute of historical or critical worth. In the brief compass of four pages 12⁰ (*Jellinek's Beth ha-Midrasch* Theil I S. 142—46. Leipzig 1853) a fabulous account is given of the conflict of the Machabeans with Antiochos and Bagris, and of their final triumph, e. g. John after a victory rears a column to commemorate his name v. 28 (Filipowski's edition is divided into seventy four verses); Judas is represented as the first born v. 51 and as dying before his father v. 58; Mattathias as sharing in the final conflict v. 60; and Eleazar while engaged in killing elephants as sinking so deeply in their dung, that he was at first invisible v. 62.

This book was originally written in Aramaic, and was designed to be read in the service of the Chanucca festival. The manuscript copies and its Hebrew translation are full of deviations and corruptions. Hoping that a comparison of the name Machabee in the different MSS. would shed some light upon the subject I sought information in regard to all the existing MSS. of this book and through the great kindness of the directors of the different libraries I am enabled to enumerate *nineteen* MSS. which contain the Megillath Antiochos. Of this number six are in England, six in Paris, four in Germany, one in Austria, one in Italy, and one is mentioned as in the possession of the late Abraham Firkowitsch.

I. Three manuscript copies of this Megilla, all on vellum, are in the **Bodleian Library at Oxford**, viz. 1) *Huntington* No. 399 (*Kennicott* 5937), with vowel points which is supposed to belong to the end of the thirteenth century; 2) *Pocock* No. 30 (*Ken.* 18) with vowel points dated the last day of Shebat

A. M. 5243 (A. D. 1483); *Opp. add.* No. 26, 4⁰ dated the 2nd of Elul A. M. 5240 (A. D. 1480).

II. **The British Museum** possesses three MSS. of the Megillath Antiochos, all of which are on vellum, viz. 1) *Harleian* No. 1861, fol. 305—306 with points, 15th century; *Harl.* No. 5713 fol. 16—17 written in London 1714, without points; *Harl.* No. 5686, written on the margin of a Roman Machsor fol. 18 and 19 without points, dated Cesena 1464.

III. **The National Library, Paris** has six manuscript copies of the Megillath Antiochos as follows; 1) No. 20 is in beautful Spanish writing on vellum by Josua ben Abraham ben Gaon A. M. 5061 (A. D. 1301). The Meg. Ant. is to be found on the last two pages in Chaldee without points. 2) No. 47 is a Spanish MS. on vellum belonging to the fourteenth century. It contains the Pentateuch, accompanied upon the upper and lower margin by the Haphtaroth, the five Megilloth, and the Meg. Ant. in Chaldee. 3) Nos. 43 and 4) 46 on vellum contain the Meg. Ant. at the end of each, in Hebrew. The latter is assigned to the fourteenth century. 5) No. 716 has the Meg. Ant. in Hebrew without vowel points, and 6) No. 130, which contains the book of Tobit, from which the edition in the London Polyglott was printed, is in Persian with Hebrew characters. [1]

IV. **The city Library, Hamburg** has a MS. No. 45 in Hebrew, on vellum, containing the Meg. Ant. with vowel points, dated A. M. 5720 (A. D. 1480).

V. **The Royal Berlin Library** purchased from Mr. Shapira of Jerusalem in 1873 two Arabico-Hebrew

---

1) For a more complete description of the Paris MSS. see "Catalogues des Manuscrits Hebreux et Samaritains de La Bibliothèque Impériale".

MSS. Nos. 627 and 629 from Yemen, which contain the Meg. Ant. folio 55ᵇ and 39ᵇ under the name מגלת בני השׁמונאי somewhat abridged, and with the old Babylonian punctuation. While these MSS. have every mark of genuineness, yet as they belong to the 16— 17th century, it is possible that the vowel points are the work of a recent hand. This is quite probable as the points themselves are incorrect, the ink with which they are written is in some cases of a different color from that of the text, and the Babylonian pointing is not supposed to belong to so late a period.[1]

VI. **In the Leipzig city Library** there is a Spanish MS. which contains the Meg. Ant. in Chaldee, on vellum, with points, of the fourteenth or fifteenth century. In the same library there is an interesting copy, No. 66, of the Codex Colbertinus (Paris No. 43), which was made by J. C. Wagenseil, on paper, and provided with a Latin translation.[2]

VII. A manuscript is in the possession of **Dr. Adolf Jellinek of Vienna**. It is on paper, is in Chaldee, furnished with vowel points and is dated 1559.

VIII. The MS. No. 111 in the **Royal Turin Library** contains the Meg. Ant. in Chaldee, without points, on vellum and is assigned to the thirteenth century.

IX. The Meg. Ant. also occurs in a fragment discovered by the Karaite Abraham Firkowitsch.

The following rare printed editions of the Megillath Antiochos are in existence in the Bodleian library

---

1) See Steinschneider's Literarische Beilage der „Heb. Bibliographie" Mai — Juni, 1873, S. 54—58. It is an interesting fact that the books of Lamentations and Esther which occur in No. 627 are on the other hand punctuated according to the Tiberian System.

1) See Wolf Bibl. Hebr. Tom. I. p. 204 and Prof. Delitzsch in the Catalogue of the City Library in Leipzig.

No. 11, Pent. Meg. Haft. Naples 1491, 4⁰; No. 19, Pent.
Meg. Haft. Constantinople 1505 folio; No. 1384 Mantua
1557, and No. 1385 Mantua 1557—9, 8⁰.

Other editions may be found as fallows: 1) In
Bartoloccii Bibliotheca Rabbinica with a Latin translation; Filipowski, *The Choice of Pearls, and the Book
of Antiochus in Aramaic, Hebrew and English*, London
1851, 32⁰; A. Jellinek's *Beth ha-Midrasch*, Leipzig
1853, Theil I, S. 142—46.

It has also been issued separately by David Sluski
under the title מגלת אנטיוכוס הנקראת מגלה יונית בשפה
ארמית ומתורגמת בלשון עברית Warschau 1864, 16⁰.

This Megillah was published by Baer Frank from
the German Jewish edition, Venice 1548, with a German translation in Hebrew characters, under the title
מגלת מתתיהו עם תרגום אשכנזי Presburg 1860, 12⁰.

Besides, this Megilla is found in a German Machsor
in a volume entitled עושה פלא Livorno 1870.

To illustrate the variations in the MSS. I give
verse 28 of the Megillath Antiochos according to Filipowski, first in Chaldee, and then in Hebrew, with the
variations of the different MSS. as follows: במתיבתיה
בה עמודה על שמיה וקרא ליה קטיל תקיפין. *Hunt.* 399 has after
וקרא ליה the name מקבי (on the margin אתר); *Poc.* 30
מקבי; *Opp. add.* 26 מקבי אתר;[1] *Harl.* 5686, f. 18ᵇ
מכבי:[2] *B. N.* No. 20, f. 467 מקבי; No. 47, f. 296 מכבי:[3]
Berlin Nos. 627 and 629 מקבי, מקבי Compare the Fac-
simile:[4] *Jellinek* מכבי with the almost illegible marginal
note מי כמוכה באלים ה' : *Turin* No. 111, f. 147ᵇ מקוי.

1) These three belong to the Bodleian library.
2) British Museum.
3) These two are in the Bibliothèque Nationale.
4) See the leaf opposite the title-page.

The above passage in the Yemen MSS. of the
Royal library in Berlin reads according to the facsimiles:

בְּמֵתַבוּתֵיהּ עֲבַד לֵיהּ בֵּיתָא וּבָא בֵּהּ מְנַרְתָּא וּקְרָא כֹּה מַקְבֵּי קְטוֹל
תְּקִיפִין׃

*On his return he built him a house and set up
therein a candlestick, and called it Makbi slayer of the
strong.* Cod. 627 gives the passage more briefly

בְּמֵתַבוּתֵיהּ בָּא מְנַרְתָּא עַל שְׁמֵיהּ וּקְרָא כֹּה מַקְבֵּי קְטוֹל תְּקִיפִין׃

I now subjoin *Filipowski's* Hebrew text of the same
verse, which is exactly that of *Harleian* No. 5713, f. 16ᵃ,
with the variations from the Hebrew MSS.: בִּשּׁוּבוֹ בָּה
עַמּוּד וַיִּקְרָא עַל שְׁמוֹ מַנְרַת הַחַזָּקִים׃ *B. N.* No. 43, f. 156
עַמּוּד עַל שְׁמוֹ וַיִּקְרָא בּוֹ מַקְבֵּי הֶרֶג הַצַּדִּיקִים; No. 46, f. 268 follows
the same order as No. 43 but has מַקְבֵּי הוֹרֵג עֲצוּמִים:
Hamburg No. 45 עַל שְׁמוֹ וַיִּקְרָא בּוֹ מִקְבֵּי הוֹרֵג הַצַּדִּיקִים. *Harl.*
No. 1861, f. 305ᵇ, 1ˢᵗ Col. וַיִּבֶן שָׁם עַמּוּד וַיִּקְרָא אֹתוֹ עֵמֶק
הֶרֶג אֲצִילִים *And he built there a pillar and called it valley
of the slaughter of the princes.*

The corruption of the surname Machabee into מִקְרַי
in the Turin MS. and into מַקְנַי in the MS. mentioned
by Firkowitsch, as well as the great variations in the
punctuation of the name show conclusively, that *it was
quite unknown in the old Jewish sources, and that it probably does not occur in Jewish literature before the age of
the so-called Jusippon ben Gurion (A. D. 940).* Hence
it is idle to quote the readings of the name in these
MSS. as authoritative, since they stand in no direct
connection with the original Hebrew book of first Machabees, but have simply been borrowed from Hellenic and
Latin sources.

Remark. I am indebted for the transcriptions of *Harl.* 1861,
f. 305ᵇ, 5686, f. 18ᵇ, 5713 f. 16ᵃ. to Prof. William Wright.

CORRECTIONS AND REMARK.

Page 4 note 1 read Ἔξω — p. 15 line 8 read *were* — p. 19 note 1 read יהוה — p. 22 note 1 read אֵיךְ — p. 31 line 11 read יְדִימֹנָה. Add to p. 11 § 4. The following remark occurs at the end of the XVI. chapter of the Arabic second book of Machabees: الى هاهنا انتهى السفر التّانى نقل العبرانيين *Thus far extends the second book as it has been taken from the Hebrews.* There is no indication in this of a Hebrew original, the remark simply means, that the Machabean history, as related in the Hebrew, that is, Jewish second book of Machabees, ends at this point, viz. the defeat of Nicanor and the festival in commemoration of it.